CITY CYCLING
BERLIN

Rapha.

Thames & Hudson

Created by Andrew Edwards and Max Leonard of
Tandem London, a design, print and editorial studio

Thanks to Mikkel Sommer for illustrations;
Katherine Hunt, *Teller* magazine, Jakob and Kasper
Padberg for city spots; and Paul Stubert for the
downlow on Berlin's racing scene

First published in the United Kingdom in 2013 by
Thames & Hudson Ltd, 181A High Holborn, London WC1V 7QX

City Cycling Berlin © 2013 Andrew Edwards and Max Leonard
Illustrations © 2013 Thames & Hudson Ltd, London and Rapha Racing Ltd

Designed by Andrew Edwards

Illustrations © 2013 Mikkel Sommer, mikkelsommer.com

British Library Cataloguing-in-Publication Data
A catalogue record for this book is available from the British Library

ISBN 978-0-500-29104-7

Printed and bound in China by Everbest Printing Co Ltd

To find out about all our publications, please visit
www.thamesandhudson.com. There you can subscribe
to our e-newsletter, browse or download our current catalogue,
and buy any titles that are in print.

CONTENTS

HOW TO USE THIS GUIDE

This Berlin volume of the *City Cycling* series is designed to give you the confidence to explore the city by bike at your own pace. On the front flaps is a locator map of the whole city to help you orient yourself. Here, you will see five neighbourhoods to explore: Mitte (p. 10); Prenzlauer Berg (p. 16); Kreuzberg and KreuzKölln (p. 22); Charlottenburg (p. 28); and Wedding (p. 34). All are easily accessible by bike, and are full of cafés, bars, galleries, museums, shops and parks. Each area is mapped in detail, and our recommendations for places of interest and where to fuel up on coffee and cake, as well as where to find a Wi-Fi connection, are marked. Take a pootle round on your bike and see what suits you.

For maps of the whole city, turn to the back. These detailed maps show bike routes across a large section of central Berlin. They'll help you navigate safely, and pinpoint everything you need, from bike shops to landmarks and more. If you fancy a set itinerary, turn to A Day On The Bike on the front flaps. It takes you on a relaxed 32km (20-mile) route through some of the parts of Berlin we haven't featured in the neighbourhood sections, and visits a few of the more touristy sights. Pick and choose the bits you fancy, go from back to front, and use the route as it suits you.

A section on Racing and Training (p. 40) fills you in pro-racing in the city and its road-cycling heritage, and provides ideas for longer rides if you want to explore the beautiful countryside around the German capital, while Essential Bike Info (p. 44) discusses road etiquette and the ins and outs of using the cycle-hire scheme and public transportation. Finally, Links and Addresses (p. 48) will give you the practical details you need to know.

BERLIN: THE CYCLING CITY

To cycle through Berlin is to pedal through a place in transformation – a transformation that has been ongoing since the reunification of Germany in 1991. It's a place that has stitched itself back together to create a political, cultural and artistic centre, where in the space of a day you might take on a hefty brunch (very important to Berliners!), before cycling off to marvel at a communist monument – then pedal over to a world-class art gallery or have a dip in a lake, before eating high-class international cuisine and experiencing some of the best nightlife in Europe. But if that sounds too busy, don't worry – it's equally possible to while away your time in a *Biergarten* or two, eating some of the famous *Currywurst* or lounging in a park.

Berlin is a mellow place where, in the summer, residents like nothing better than to chill out in one of the many green spaces. It's one of the greenest cities around – as if a small city were stretched out to fit a much larger footprint and the resulting gaps filled in with trees and parks. Everywhere you go there is a welcome sense of space. You'll probably cycle relatively longer distances here compared with what you might be used to at home, but you won't notice it since progress is so pleasant, quick and hassle-free. Although there are plenty of cars on the roads, it's obvious as soon as you arrive that this is a city where everybody is on their bike. Cycling is very safe, and it's a pleasure to get around by bike – though do note the distances involved, and refer to the times indicated on our maps. Drivers are on the whole courteous and aware of cyclists, wherever they meet, but most of the time you won't have to.

The Allied bombings of the city in the Second World War, together with the Communists' postwar desire for pomp and circumstance, mean that roads and pavements are extremely wide, and the views when cycling down Karl-Marx-Allee, Unter den Linden or parts of Charlottenburg evoke a real sense of grandeur. Taking advantage of all the space, the city's planners often thought to equip the long boulevards with handsome segregated bike lanes, paved in a different sort of brick, which share space with pedestrians, rather than motorized traffic. They're the product of a regeneration plan from 2004 that promoted an environmentally friendly approach to transport and addressed mobility issues for Berliners, opening up one-way and dead-end streets for cyclists, integrating cycling with public transport and encouraging councils and housing associations to provide bicycle parking.

A further bonus: the city is virtually pan-flat. Most of the time, the roads stay close in height to the river Spree, which meanders through the fertile, low-lying plateau on which Berlin is built. Do not use the river for navigation, as its serpentine bends will confuse; the several canals, such as the Landwehrkanal, which bisects Kreuzberg, are more reliable. Also more useful are landmarks, including the Reichstag (see A Day On The Bike) and Hauptbahnhof; the Fernsehturm (also in A Day On The Bike), the TV tower near Alexanderplatz in the heart of the old East, in particular dominates the skyline and is an almost constant point of reference. These days, around Potsdamer Platz, at the southeastern tip of the huge, leafy Tiergarten (p. 29), there's a clutch of flashy modern offices belonging to multinationals, which is also handy to navigate by. But it's the Fernsehturm that makes the biggest impression: it's an omnipresent reminder of the city's history, just as the varied architecture you'll encounter while pedalling around subtly reminds you at every turn of the momentous events Berlin has lived through.

There's far, far more to the city than its history, though. Berliners don't live in the past, and visitors don't have to either. Get on your bike and discover the creative, cosmopolitan, relaxed, ethnically diverse place that welcomes and rewards exploration.

NEIGHBOURHOODS

MITTE
HISTORY, SHOPPING AND GALLERIES

Mitte (literally, 'middle') is Berlin's old-fashioned central neighbourhood, bounded by the Tiergarten (p. 29) in the west, Alexanderplatz in the east, Nordbahnhof in the north and Checkpoint Charlie (see A Day On The Bike) in the south – more or less the course of the Berlin Wall, in fact. Before the Second World War, Mitte was the centre of a culturally vibrant city; later, scarred by division, it became the western edge of East Berlin. After two decades of regeneration and gentrification, it is difficult to see the Wall's former course – but keep your eye on the ground in front of you as you pedal, as it is marked out with a double-row of cobblestones on the roads and pavements it once cut across.

It's a miraculous transformation, except, perhaps, for <u>Potsdamer Platz</u>. Once the epicentre of outrageous Weimar café culture, the square was flattened in the bombing and, after 1945, was no-man's-land between East and West. It's where, so the saying goes, some of the world's best architects – Renzo Piano, Helmut Jahn, Richard Rogers – did some of their worst work, and a modern no-man's-land it remains. If you are in the central and western corners of Mitte, we recommend the **DDR Museum** ①, a former 'European museum of the year', which gives visitors a taste of daily life in the Deutsche Demokratische Republik. For more of Mitte's historical sights and museums, turn to A Day On The Bike; here, we'll concentrate on the northeastern part of the area, in and around <u>Rosa-Luxemburg-Platz</u>, where the locals and visitors to the rejuvenated Mitte come to eat, drink, shop and relax.

First stop, **Buchhandlung Walther König** ②, a specialist art and photography bookshop just behind the interesting **Hackescher Markt** ③, an old market square now known for its nightlife. Walther König also has a branch in the **Hamburger Bahnhof** ④, which today houses the National Gallery's museum of contemporary art. Also close to Hackescher Markt is the **Buchstabenmuseum** ⑤ (museum of typography), or for cutting-edge arts, crafts and design, head to the **Direktorenhaus** ⑥, near Alexanderplatz. For fashion, head to **Apartment** ⑦; hidden downstairs under some gallery space, it's almost an installation in its own right. **Yuu Shop** ⑧, meanwhile, sells clothes from the previous season's collection by European designers such as Dries Van Noten and Martin Margiela. If you don't mind buying your winter wardrobe in summer, grab a bargain.

For design, make your way to **The Early Bird Hype** ⑨, a bold and colourful store that often hosts photography exhibitions. Just down the road is **Do You Read Me?!** ⑩, which stocks a great range of books and international art and design magazines. With less emphasis on magazines, another bookstore, **Pro QM** ⑪, has one of the largest selections of architecture, art and photography books. **Gestalten Space** ⑫ mixes gallery space with a bookshop, while **Me Collectors Room** ⑬ in Auguststraße is one of the city's newest homes for art, and features the private collection of Thomas Olbricht, with works from the sixteenth century through to the twenty-first. There are many private galleries in this area: **Neugerriemschneider** ⑭ is one of the most prominent, representing international names such as Ólafur Elíasson; and **Galerie Christian Nagel** ⑮ is also well established. The former department store-turned-art squat **Kunsthaus Tacheles** ⑯, located on <u>Oranienburger Straße</u>, is a reminder of the area's bohemian past. Once housing painters' and sculptors' studios, as well as an evolving collection of their work (of variable quality), it is now closed and the residents displaced for redevelopment. Catch this architectural landmark while it's still there.

For food in the area, **Cocolo** ⑰ makes a great Japanese ramen soup, or for something more traditional (and stodgy), try the perennial favourite **Schwarzwaldstuben** ⑱, which serves Swabian cuisine from southern Germany – think great schnitzels, potatoes and beer. And for drinking near the galleries and shops, try **Bar 3** ⑲ or **Clärchens Ballhaus** ⑳, an old-time dancehall and ballroom with a beautiful garden. For an upmarket end to the day, seek out **Tausend** ㉑, a chic, sleek designer bar with no sign, hidden across town under the railway arches.

REFUELLING

FOOD
Babanbè ㉒ is a smart *bánh mì* (Vietnamese sandwich) fusion place

DRINK
Strandbad-Mitte ㉓ is a traditional bar with a sunny terrace

WI-FI
Sankt Oberholz ㉔ is a home from home for Berlin's freelancers

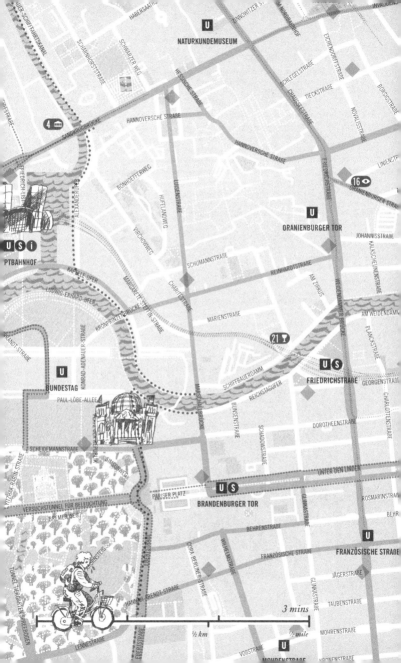

ROSENTHALER PLATZ  U

24

ZEHDENICKER STRAßE

LOTTUMSTRAße

SAARBROCKER ST

TORSTRAße

3 14 23 13 20 10 17 12 8

ROSA-LUXEMBURG-PL. U

11 19 15 9 7

WEINMEISTERSTRAße U

HACKESCHER MARKT 3 S

2

5

ALEXANDERPLATZ U S

1

KLOSTERSTRAße U

6

MÄRKISCHES MUSEUM U

HAUSVOGTEIPLATZ

WALLSTRAße

U WALLSTRAße

PRENZLAUER BERG
STREET LIFE, VINTAGE, BOUTIQUES AND BRUNCHES

Schickimicki is the not-entirely-complimentary adjective some locals use for Prenzlauer Berg. It translates to something like 'yuppie' in English, or 'bobo' in French. Unification attracted squats and a bohemian crowd to the area, which has since been slowly gentrified. But don't let that put you off: the wide, leafy roads, boutiques, squares and *Altbau* apartments (traditional housing stock, with the most coveted buildings dating from between 1850 and 1920) are pleasant to pedal around. It's found northeast of Mitte, across Torstraße, and bounded by Brunnenstraße to the west and Prenzlauer Allee to the east.

On the western side, you'll find two contrasting parks. **Mauerpark** ① is quite windswept, but contains a section of the Wall high on a

hill; it also hosts a flea market on Sundays with impromptu open-air karaoke that draws quite a crowd. To the south is the more genteel **Volkspark am Weinbergsweg** ②, with a pretty flower garden and a Swiss chalet-style café, **Nola's am Weinberg** ③, perched on a hill in the middle. In between the two is Arkonaplatz, where you can find the **Trödelmarkt Arkonaplatz** ④ on Sundays, with vintage articles from the 1950s and '60s. **Paul's Boutique** ⑤ on Oderberger Straße in the French Quarter (developed after the Franco–Prussian war, with streets named after French towns), is a quintessential Prenzlauer Berg vintage shop, with distressed cast-offs and sneakers piled around a boom box (try sister shop **Goo** ⑥, as well as **Memory Vintage** ⑦ for more upmarket second-hand clothes). It's close to **Kastanienallee** ⑧, known colloquially as 'Casting-alley' for the beautiful people that stroll up and down it. It's worth a few circuits to take it all in. You'll find record stores **Franz & Josef** ⑨ and **Melting Point** ⑩ in Kastanienallee itself, and in the environs homewares at **Liv Emaille** ⑪, retro glasses at **optiKing** ⑫, hats at **Heimat** ⑬, street fashion at **Le Gang** ⑭ or **Who Killed Bambi?** ⑮, and much more.

Afterwards, stop off at **Prater Garten** ⑯, Berlin's oldest *Biergarten*, for a Prater Pils or a Schwarzebier. Or if all this consumption is too much, the **Stiftung Haus der Geschichte der BRD** ⑰ presents a selection of industrial design and objects to illustrate everyday life in East Germany. It's in the **Kulturbrauerei** ⑱, a handsome red-brick former brewery, now full of cafés, bars and sustainable businesses, as well as the recommended **Berlin on Bike** ⑲ hire shop. Cycle away from the bustle of the main thoroughfares, and life in Prenzlauer Berg steps down a gear. **Helmholtzplatz** ⑳ is a nice park, and at the centre of *Schickimicki* brunch-land. **Kollwitzplatz** ㉑ is the scene of an enticing farmers' market on Saturdays and a quieter organic market on Thursdays; the weird towers atop the reservoir are home to sound art installations in the summer, thanks to the

Singuhr-Hörgalerie ㉒. Descend into the brick tunnels for some aural treats. Just down <u>Kollwitzstraße</u> is **Meierei** ㉓, a tiny but beautifully restored bistro that serves Alpine specialities – think sausages, cheese, bread and, of course, apple strudel. Finally, road cycling fans should head north to **Cicli Berlinetta** ㉔, full of classic bikes, frames and components. Real *tifosi* are advised to grab a double espresso at **No Fire, No Glory!** ㉕ on the way.

REFUELLING

FOOD	DRINK
Kaffeehaus Sowohlalsauch ㉖, for good brunches, coffee and cake	Fleischmöbel ㉘ is an atmospheric after-work bar of choice
White Trash ㉗ for Asian kitsch, rock 'n' roll cabaret and brilliant cheeseburgers	Bonanza Coffee Heroes ㉙ is a must-visit for coffee snobs

WI-FI
St Gaudy ㉚ has Wi-Fi, coffee, yoga classes, tango, and more

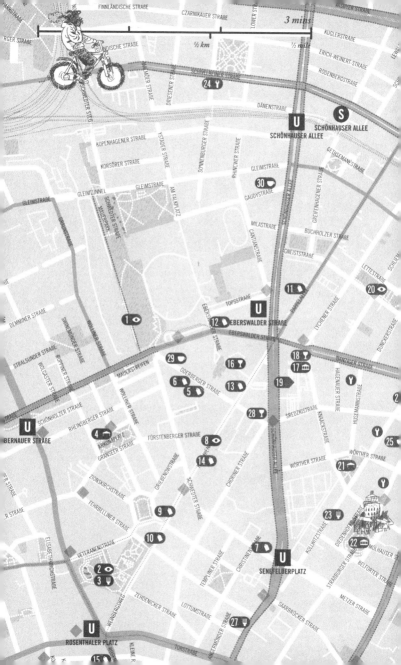

KREUZBERG & KREUZKÖLLN

VIBRANT AND LAID-BACK CITY LIVING

Kreuzberg, south of the Mitte, was only thus christened and incorporated into Berlin in 1920. In less than a hundred years, it has had many lives: a densely populated area filled with industry (particularly printing); an impoverished enclave of West Berlin; and now a vibrant, laid-back multicultural neighbourhood, with a large attendant population of artists and creatives – and a few freeloaders, too. SO36 ① , a club named after Kreuzberg's main postcode and famously a hangout for Iggy Pop and Davie Bowie (who lived on Hauptstraße, in Schöneberg), is on one of the area's main drags, <u>Oranienstraße</u>. To the southeast, Kreuzberg shades into Neukölln, an up-and-coming neighbourhood, and the borders between the two are called 'KreuzKölln' by some. It's this eastern section that is the cooler, more punky area; to the west, towards Schöneberg, the SO61 postcode is much more genteel.

The area we're talking about here starts south of Checkpoint Charlie. Begin at **Martin-Gropius-Bau** ②, originally the home of the city's museum of applied arts and now an exhibition hall, or the **Berlinische Galerie** ③, which presents Berlin's history with artistic contributions from famous native sons including George Grosz. Nearby, architect Daniel Libeskind's addition to the **Jewish Museum** ④ is an impressive and moving space. Also on this northern edge is **Solar** ⑤, a fifteenth-floor bar where the CIA top brass used to meet for cocktails and keep an eye on the city. It's still a good vantage point for spying on city life, though it does get busy. Stay in SO61 and head south, taking in **Kühn Keramik** ⑥, a quirky artist-run ceramics showroom, and towards **Viktoriapark** ⑦, which has a spectacular 20m (66-ft) high waterfall and the hill – *Kreuzberg* – after which the area is named.

Stop off at **Vanille & Marille** ⑧ for an ice cream to take with you, or **Barcomi's** ⑨, a 1950s-style café with diner favourites (bagels, cheesecake); it sits on Bergmannstraße, a lively road to pedal down. You're a long way south here, and you could cycle east along the *Landwehrkanal*, a laid-back trail lined with cafés and the **Maybachufer food market** ⑩. **Sing Blackbird** ⑪, a vintage clothes shop and café, is also close by. Or cycle up to Oranienstraße and the Moritzplatz U-bahn station, where you'll find **Modulor** ⑫ for stationery and art supplies, and the café **Betahaus** ⑬, a multi-use space that holds art and design events. Be sure to visit **Prinzessinnengarten** ⑭ too, a community garden, salvaged from wasteland by locals, with a mellow café in the middle. Further down the road you'll find the **Museum der Dinge** ⑮ ('museum of things'), an archive of product design and homewares from the twentieth century.

This eastern end of Oranienstraße is prime brunching territory. A favourite spot is **Bateau Ivre** ⑯, named after a Rimbaud poem; the food is good and the service relaxed. **Morena Bar** ⑰ is also a contender, while **Jolesch** ⑱, around the corner, serves brilliant schnitzel. Moving into KreuzKölln, Falckensteinstraße, Weserstraße

and <u>Reuterstraße</u> all have relaxed cafés in the day and busy bars at night. If you're not catching the sun's last rays at Bateau Ivre, try **KaterHolzig** ⑲, a hip bar and restaurant in a derelict riverside warehouse, or **Bellman** ⑳ for distressed chic and brilliant cocktails. **Arena** ㉑ is the destination for clubbers; it's next to **Badeschiff** ㉒, a shipping container-turned-lido, floating in the Spree. In the winter it becomes a sauna, with a semi-enclosed pool. On the way is **Keirin Cycle Culture Café** ㉓, a bike shop and café run by followers of the Japanese track-racing discipline. Expect beautiful old bikes and plenty to look at on the walls.

REFUELLING

FOOD	DRINK
The popular Italian **Molinari & Ko** ㉔ looks after you from breakfast espresso to dinner al fresco	**Johann Rose** ㉕, out east, serves up great coffee

WI-FI
Bully's Bakery ㉖ – share coffee, pastries and Wi-Fi with Bully, the resident dog
East London ㉗ will serve you a British fry-up while you surf

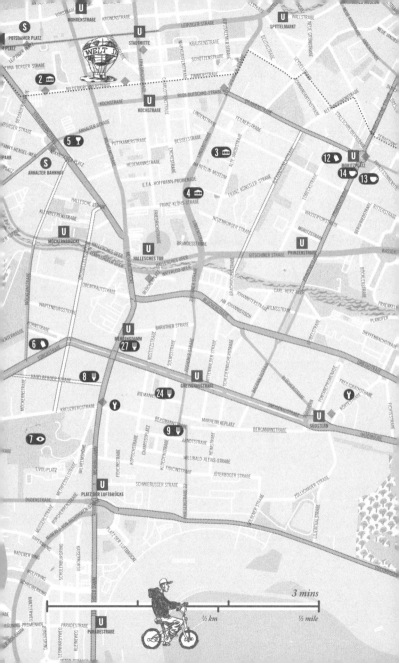

If you've been spending time in the grittier Kreuzberg or the trendier Prenzlauer Berg, then Charlottenburg, Berlin's sprawling western neighbourhood, can feel like a completely different city. Its quiet back streets provide an alternative to the 'alternative', while the Kurfürstendamm has all the large international shops that the former East conspicuously lacks. The Ku'damm, as it's known, is in the south of the area we'll be exploring here, while the western reaches of the Spree are in the north.

Cycle through the **Tiergarten** ①, the huge, wooded park where Berliners run, cycle, picnic and unwind, not missing the **Charlottenburger Tor flea market** ② at the weekends. Tucked away in a dingy street behind the Zoologischer Garten S-Bahn station is the **Museum für Fotografie** ③, well worth a visit, or cycle past the **Kaiser Wilhelm Memorial Church** ④ on Breitscheidplatz; its ruined spire has been left as it was after the church was bombed in 1943. Just down the road is the **Käthe Kollwitz Museum** ⑤, dedicated to the German Expressionist painter and sculptor. Its garden is connected to that of the **Literaturhaus** ⑥, where you can catch up on your German literature and have *Kaffee und Kuchen* at the Café Wintergarten. Aside from the shops, there's not much to do down the Ku'damm, so head north to Kantstraße, Berlin's main area for design and interiors showrooms, and also home to **Paris Bar** ⑦, a legendary bistro and hangout of artists and celebrities, with walls adorned with art amassed by the painter Martin Kippenberger. Aside from the bar's neon sign, the area's sophistication is understated and the picturesque **Savignyplatz** ⑧ is the jewel in its crown.

In the arches under the U-Bahn, among the restaurants and cafés, you'll find **Bücherbogen am Savignyplatz** ⑨, an amazing bookshop specializing in architecture, where it's easy to lose track of time. Follow the arches either way along the **railway** ⑩ and you'll find independent furniture and homeware boutiques, and lots of interesting windows to peer in. Nearby is **Art + Industry** ⑪, one of Berlin's best vintage furniture dealers, born out of a restoration business. The showroom is on Bleibtreustraße, which, along with Schlüterstraße, is a pleasant road to cycle down, lined with trees and restaurants. Also close by is **Galerie Camera Work** ⑫, which exhibits photography by Man Ray, Helmut Newton and the like, as well as work by up-and-coming stars.

When you've had your fill around Kantstraße, head up into residential Charlottenburg, via **Alt-Lietzow** ⑬, the historic centre of the neighbourhood, and <u>Wilmersdorfer Straße</u>, an old-school residential and shopping street, where you'll find **Sportantiquariat Matthias Drummer** ⑭, a book dealer specializing in sports books. In the very northwest is the eighteenth-century **Charlottenburg Palace** ⑮, a beautiful Baroque residence built for Sophie Charlotte (after whom the area is named), wife of Friedrich III. It began as a summer palace, but plans got out of hand. (It's not surprising the emperor almost bankrupted the German state.) Opposite is the **Sammlung Scharf-Gerstenberg** ⑯, a state-owned collection of artworks by the Surrealists and their antecedents, housed in the palace's grandiose former stable block. Finally, if you fancy a longer pedal, follow Kantstraße to its end (about 2km, or 1.2 miles) and you'll reach **Lietzensee** ⑰, a picturesque small lake (with café and terrace) within easy reach of the city centre.

REFUELLING

FOOD

Rogacki ⑱ is a traditional Polish deli, reportedly making two tons of potato salad a week

KaDeWe ⑲, Berlin's upmarket department store, has amazing cafés, oyster bars and food halls

DRINK

Schwarzes Café ⑳ is open 24 hours a day, serving drinks and good, simple food to night owls

WI-FI

Café Das Muntermacher ㉑ is bright and airy, and **My Cheesecake** ㉒ will serve you cheesecake and more while you surf

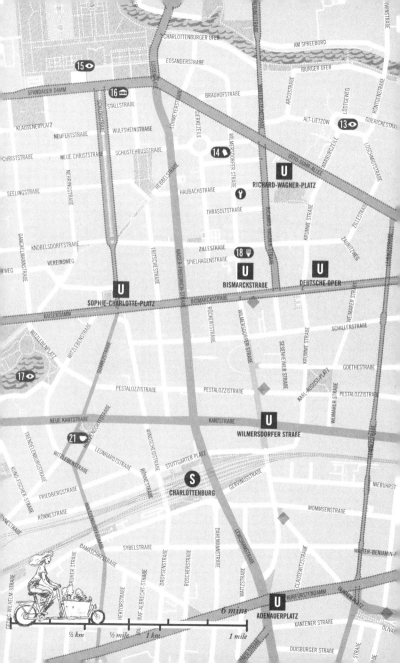

There was a time when the northern boroughs of Berlin weren't as enticing as Prenzlauer Berg or as vibrant as Kreuzberg. They are still quieter and more residential, but, as other areas change and become more expensive, populations and attractions are shifting. Wedding is still a working-class district on the whole, and feels less metropolitan than other parts of the city, but the area is well worth a trip – for the architecture, galleries, brew pubs and more.

When we're talking about Wedding here, we're looking at the district north of <u>Bernauer Straße</u>, west of Brunnenstraße and east of the Berlin-Spandau ship canal (see below). Bernauer Straße was once an infamous barrier between West and East, the scene of many tunnel escapes and desperate tragedies as people leapt from the windows of buildings along the road (in the East) to the pavement below (in the French sector of the West). It's now the site of the **Berlin Wall Memorial** ① (*Gedenkstätte Berliner Mauer*), a sensitive yet chilling reminder of the wall's ominous presence. Travel up past the incredibly huge former **AEG wartime factories** ② on Hussitenstraße (a turbine hall still stands on Huttenstraße in the Moabit neighbourhood, too) and you'll reach the **Volkspark Humboldthain** ③, a popular green spot with a hill made of wartime rubble that gives a fantastic view of the city. There's also a flak tower left over from the war, and a lido. Not far away is the **Anti-Kriegs-Museum** ④, founded by an anarchist in 1925 in response to the First World War.

Another way of travelling north into Wedding is along <u>Heidestraße</u>, an industrial stretch of road that now also hosts galleries, events and pop-ups. Take a ride up there and keep your eyes peeled, as some of the venues can be quite ephemeral. Heidestraße also leads nicely to the path alongside the **Berlin-Spandau Ship Canal** ⑤, which takes you through greenery, past factories and eventually to **Plötzensee** ⑥, perhaps the most accessible of Berlin's famous lakes, to which the whole city appears to decamp at weekends during the summer. Swim anywhere around the lake, not just at the **Freibad** ⑦, although this does have a café and child-friendly facilities. Elsewhere in Wedding, art-wise, there's **Stattbad Wedding** ⑧, a studio space-cum-gallery in a mostly intact former municipal swimming pool building. **Galerie Max Hetzler** ⑨, which exhibits artists such as Jeff Koons, Bridget Riley and Rineke Dijkstra, is in an interesting mixed-use building in central Wedding, along with other Berlin galleries.

Other than that, cruise around and enjoy the small-town atmosphere – heading up <u>Ostenderstraße</u>, <u>Genterstraße</u> and <u>Schulstraße</u>, for example, or follow the tiny and little-known Panke river to the **Luisenbad Library** ⑩, a former public baths that still has some impressive mosaics. To the west and slightly north is the **Afrikanische Viertel** ⑪, or African Quarter, a collection of roads named after African countries that is now noted for its Modernist housing estates. Built between 1910 and 1933, they were added to the UNESCO list of world heritage sites in 2008. Take a ride around the neat streets and spot architectural works by **Bruno Taut** ⑫, **Jean Krämer** ⑬, **Mies van der Rohe** ⑭ and others – there are handy information panels dotted around **Schillerpark** ⑮ to help you find them.

Just north is another interesting development: the **Gartenkolonie Freudental** ⑯ – allotment-style gardens on state land, immaculately tended, with vegetables, fruit, flowers and rustic wooden houses. If that's too homely, **Berliner Unterwelten** ⑰ will take you somewhere completely different: it runs tours that explore Berlin's bunkers and

underground infrastructure, exposing the dark secrets of the past within. After that, you probably deserve a beer – try **Hausbrauerei Eschenbräu** ⑱, a traditional German brew pub.

REFUELLING

FOOD	DRINK
Korea Haus ⑲ may be an unlikely spot, but it serves great food	**Coffee Star** ⑳ does exactly what it says **Lindengarten** ㉑ is a nice, tranquil *Biergarten*

WI-FI
TassenKuchen ㉒ will get you connected

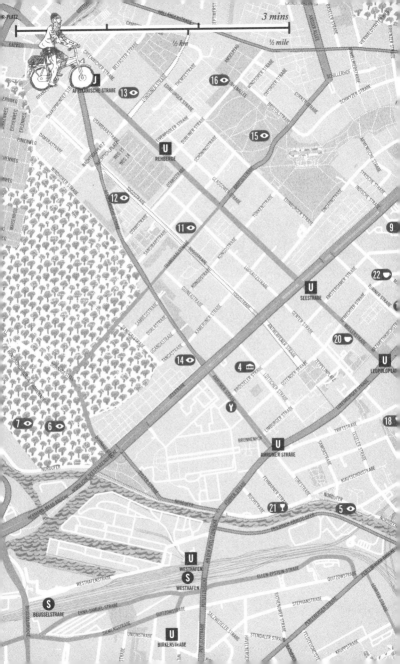

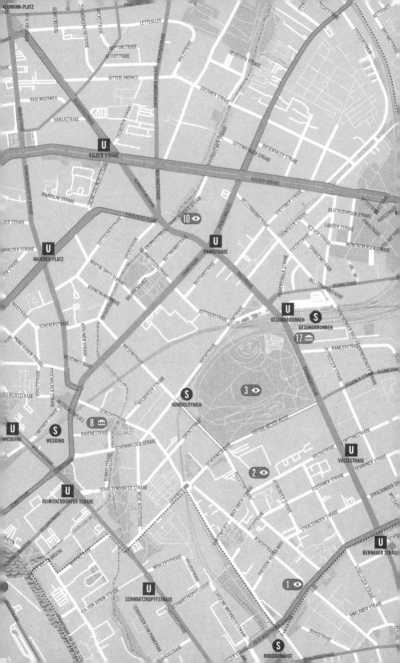

RACING AND TRAINING

Like so much in postwar Berlin, the city's racing past, until reunification, consists of two parallel but separate streams. In truth, cycle sport had never taken hold in Germany the way it did in Belgium or France, but during the years of the DDR the ruling party saw sport as a propaganda tool – both to boost morale among the masses and to show superiority externally – and cycling was placed firmly in the spotlight. The Peace Race was born in 1948 and, from 1950 included Berlin in its axis of communist capital stage stops (the others being Warsaw and Prague). It subsequently established itself as the major stage race of the Soviet Bloc, and was last run in 2006, well after the fall of Communism. There were no 'professional' athletes in the East, and when Western cyclists penetrated the Iron Curtain to compete (the Scottish clubman Ian Steel won in 1952), they found the East German 'amateurs' to be fearsome full-time athletes, well trained and supported by the state. Since many did not leave the country, and none could ride in pro races, their impact was limited on the road.

For such a small country, however, East Germany had racked up an impressive number of Olympic medals (although, sadly, a history of state-endorsed doping and chemical experimentation has been revealed across many East German sports), and after the Berlin Wall came down, these high-class amateurs flooded into the professional market. Cycling luminaries Jens Voigt, Jan Ullrich and Erik Zabel were among those who grew up in, and survived, Berlin's sports-focused school system. Also in Berlin was the Institut für Forschung und Entwicklung von Sportgeräten (FES), the state's R&D centre for sports equipment. FES made the first-ever carbon disc wheel, and the German national team to this day still rides FES bikes. In nearby Zossen is the **Radsport-Museum Wünsdorf**, which commemorates East Germany's cycling history. Full of memorabilia and old bikes, it's around 40km (25 miles) from the centre of town, so is a manageable cycle out. For a route, plus other training routes out of Berlin, check our Links and Addresses section (p. 48).

Zossen was also the start and end of the Rund um Berlin, which formed a complete loop around Berlin and was Germany's oldest cycling race. First held in 1896, the race has been won by all the biggest names in German cycling; only two non-Germans were ever victorious. It was last run in 2008, but Erik Zabel, a proud Berliner, recently established the ProRace, a fledgling road race that has been won by Marcel Kittel and André Greipel. Not quite a resurrection of the Rund, the ProRace takes place in July as part of the **Velothon Berlin**, during which amateurs race a closed-road sportive through the Brandenburger Tor and other sights in the heart of the capital. Other than Zabel and Jens Voigt, who still lives in Berlin and belongs to the prestigious **Berliner TSC** cycling club, Paul Martens grew up here; and, on the other side of the Wall, East Berliners could count Jürgen Geschke, Gustav-Adolf 'Täve' Schur and Volker Winkler among their stars. These days, Berlin is still home to the country's track elite: Maximilian Levy, Robert Förstemann and Robert Bartko live in the region, and the **Berlin Six Day**, held in January, is a beer-fuelled celebration of track cycling. In 1987 the Tour de France started in West Berlin, in the shadow of the Brandenburger Tor, and the organizers of the Giro d'Italia are talking about a Berlin start before 2020.

For training, Berlin is of such a size that if you want a short ride, it's probably best to stay within the city limits: a popular thing to do is to ride the runways at **Tempelhofer Freiheit**, a former airport turned public park. If you want to go further afield, the Grunewald to the southwest is the place to start. Many local clubs meet at the western end of Spanische Allee on Saturdays: a slow ride leaves at 9:30am and a fast ride at 10 – you might even see Jens. A good alternative for easy or fast group rides are the **RTF**s (*Radtourenfahrten*), in which about 40 to 100 people head out for anything between 80 to 180km (50 to 112 miles). The goal is to get your card stamped at the different food zones on the way, so, strictly speaking, it's not a race, and you can pick your riding companions according to how your legs are feeling.

For spares and repairs, **Radsport Heinze** is a traditional shop between Neukölln and Treptow, run by three generations of the Heinze family, which specializes in Italian bikes and parts. **Rad-Kreuz** in Kreuzberg is good for shoes and gear and is strong in cyclo-cross, and counts ex-German champion Philipp Walsleben among its former employees. Both, though not ostensibly hire places, might be able to help you out with a bike. Alternatively, try **Pino Touren** for your Velothon steed. **Villa Pasculli**, meanwhile, is a little outside the city centre and is a beautiful bike boutique that also serves good coffee. It's an ideal stop after a Grunewald ride, as is **Café Médoc**. In the centre of town, racers often head to the authentically Italian **Giro d'Espresso** in Charlottenburg for a pick-me-up before or after training.

RACING AND TRAINING

ESSENTIAL BIKE INFO

Cycling in Berlin is very civilized, but here are a few guidelines to keep you rolling along smoothly.

ETIQUETTE

- Always indicate when turning, so that people cycling behind you are aware that you're slowing down and changing direction
- Most bike lanes are integrated into the pavement space, rather than the road, so be doubly vigilant about pedestrians
- Equally, don't stray into the bike lanes when you're walking – pedestrians in Berlin are well trained and stay out of the way
- Cycle on the right-hand side of the bike lane, so people can overtake you
- Generally, people will stop at red lights
- If you ride a fixed-wheel bike, be sure that it has a hand brake on it. It's illegal not to have one, and the police have been known to stop and fine – or confiscate bikes from – riders that don't

SAFETY

Berlin is a safe city to cycle in. The wide streets more often than not provide a bike lane, and local drivers, if they're driving across a bike lane, will generally be aware of cyclists and courteously let them through. Nevertheless:

- Make sure that you are aware of what the traffic is doing, as some bike paths will take you from separated space to shared space with little warning, especially around traffic lights
- Berlin's taxis drive erratically and fast, so keep an eye out for them
- Watch out for tram tracks, which can catch your wheel and become slippery when wet. Berlin's tram system is less extensive than, say, Amsterdam's, so it's almost more of a surprise when you encounter the clattering trams

SECURITY

Berlin, like many cities, has a problem with bicycle theft, and you shouldn't leave a bike unlocked, even for a minute. Your hire bike should come with a chain lock, and we recommend using it to tie the bike to something immovable if you're going to leave it unattended. If you're riding a nice or valuable bike, it's essential to use a good lock and to consider locking the wheels, too, so that opportunist bike thieves will pick an easier target. Take your cues from locals: if you don't see any nice bikes locked in the vicinity, it's probably best not to leave yours.

FINDING YOUR WAY

There is a good system of signposts on Berlin's bike routes, and, once you have a basic geography of the city, the roadsigns are helpful too. With lots of long, straight roads, it's easy to cover a lot of ground quickly, without stopping to consult a map too much. U-Bahn and S-Bahn stations are relatively spaced out compared with other cities, but they do make good landmarks.

CITY BIKES AND BIKE HIRE

Berlin is full of bike-hire places, and many hotels and hostels have bikes to hire. If they don't take your fancy, there are shops on every other street, even outside of tourist areas. We recommend **Faltrad Direktor** in Charlottenburg, or **Berlin On Bike** (p. 18) in the Kulturbrauerei in Prenzlauer Berg, which also does bike tours.

Berlin, in common with other German cities, has a municipal bike-hire scheme, run by Deutsche Bahn, called **Call A Bike**; you'll see the red bikes at stations around the capital. Once you've registered (by phone or online – though phone may be easier, since the website is in German only, and most Germans speak good English), following the on-screen instructions at the docking stations is straightforward. If you travel frequently to German cities, it might be a good idea to sign up. It costs 8Ø¢ a minute, up to a maximum of €15 a day. If you're just going to Berlin for a break, however, it may be more convenient to hire one elsewhere.

OTHER PUBLIC TRANSPORT

German buses do not accept bikes, though you can, with a bicycle ticket, take a bike on the U- and S-Bahn. On the U-Bahn, they're not allowed between 6 and 9am, or 2 and 5pm, but you can take them on the S-Bahn at any time. The appropriate carriages have bicycle illustrations on the windows, and it's two per carriage at most.

TRAVELLING TO BERLIN WITH BIKES

Berlin, being a long way east, isn't brilliantly served by international trains from Western Europe. Although there are overnight services to Amsterdam, Paris, Zurich, Vienna and Budapest, daily services west tend to connect to the international network via Cologne. You can get to Cologne from the UK on **Eurostar** (via Brussels) and **Thalys** train services; on Eurostar you should, as of 2013, put your bike in a bag and send it via the registered baggage service. This costs £10 each way for the 'Turn Up and Go' service, where you leave your bike bag at a counter in the check-in hall.

One point to note is that German ICE high-speed trains (see the **Deutsche Bahn** website) will not allow bike bags bigger than 85cm (33 in.) in any dimension, which practically rules out any non-folding bikes. You can take a bike in a bag on the slower Intercity and Eurocity (IC and EC) trains, which also allow bikes to be wheeled on board if you pay for a reservation. It's best to take your bike in a bag on any other country's trains towards Germany, and then factor in a non high-speed train onwards from Cologne if you're intending to travel this way to Berlin.

At some point in 2014, Berlin's much-delayed **Brandenburg Willy Brandt Airport** will open, replacing the existing Tegel and Schönefeld airports. It will be located about 18km (11 miles) south of the city centre. Tegel and Schönefeld are as close, if not closer, so they are all cyclable, if you're feeling adventurous. Bike lanes pass near both the existing airports, and finding your way into the city centre shouldn't be too difficult, but we'd recommend buying a very good map for the way back, so you don't risk missing your flight!

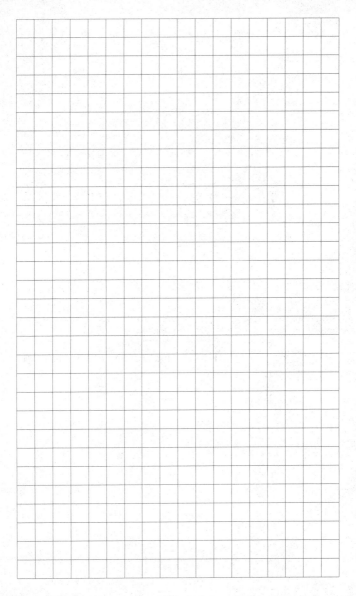

LINKS AND ADDRESSES

Anti-Kriegs-Museum
Brüsseler Straße 21, 13353
anti-kriegs-museum.de

Apartment
Memhardstraße 8, 10178B
apartmentberlin.de

Arena
Eichenstraße 4, 12435
arena-berlin.de

Art + Industry
Bleibtreustraße 40, 10623
aiberlin.de

Babanbè
Tucholskystraße 18–20, 10117
babanbe.com

Babette
Karl-Marx-Allee 36, 10178
barbabette.com

Badeschiff
Eichenstraße 4, 12435
arena-berlin.de/badeschiff

Barcomi's
Bergmannstraße 21, 10961
barcomis.de

Barini
Böhmische Straße 46, 12055
barini-nk.de

Bar 3
Weydingerstraße 20, 10178

Bateau Ivre
Core Tex Records 18, 10997

Bauhaus Archive
Klingelhöferstraße 14, 10785
bauhaus.de

Bellman
Reichenberger Straße 103, 10999

Berliner Philharmonie
Herbert-von-Karajan-Straße
1, 10785
berliner-philharmoniker.de

Berliner TSC
Paul-Heyse-Straße 25, 10407
berlinertsc.de

Berliner Unterwelten
Brunnenstraße 105, 13355
berliner-unterwelten.de

Berlinische Galerie
Alte Jakobstraße 124, 10969
berlinischegalerie.de

Berlin Wall Memorial
Bernauer Straße 111, 13355
berliner-mauer-gedenkstaette.de

Berlin Zoo
Hardenbergplatz 8, 10787
zoo-berlin.de

Betahaus
Prinzessinnenstraße 19°20, 10969
betahaus.de

Bonanza Coffee Heroes
Oderberger Straße 35, 10435
bonanzacoffee.de

Brandenburger Tor
Pariser Platz, 10117
berlin.de

Bücherbogen am Savignyplatz
Stadtbahnbogen 593, 10623
buecherbogen.com

Buchhandlung Walther König
Burgstraße 27, 10178
buchhandlung-walther-koenig.de

Buchstabenmuseum
Karl-Liebknecht-Straße 13,
10178
buchstabenmuseum.de

Bully's Bakery
Friedelstraße 7, 12047
bullysbakery.com

Café Das Muntermacher
Suarezstraße 46, 14057
das-muntermacher.de

Café Médoc
Am Fuchsbau 33, 14532
cafemedoc.de

Café Moskau
Karl-Marx-Allee 34, 10178
cafemoskau.com

Café Opernpalais
Unter den Linden 5–7, 10117

**Charlottenburger Tor
flea market**
Straße des 17. Juni 100, 10557
berliner-troedelmarkt.de

Charlottenburg Palace
Spandauer Damm 20–24, 14059
spsg.de

Checkpoint Charlie
Friedrichstraße 43–45, 10117
berlin.de

Clärchens Ballhaus
Auguststraße 24, 10117
ballhaus.de

Coffee Star
Müllerstraße 146, 13353
coffeestar.net

Cocolo
Gipsstraße 3, 10119
oliverprestele.de

Dachkammer
Simon-Dach-Straße 39, 10245
dachkammer.com

DDR Museum
Karl-Liebknecht-Straße 1, 10178
ddr-museum.de

Direktorenhaus
Am Krögel 2, 10179
direktorenhaus.com

Do You Read Me?!
Auguststraße 28, 10117
doyoureadme.de

East London
Mehringdamm 33, 10961
eastlondon.de

East Side Gallery
Mühlenstraße, 10243
eastsidegallery.com

Fernsehturm
Panoramastraße 1a, 10178
tv-turm.de

Fleischmöbel Bar
Oderberger Straße 2, 10435

Franz & Josef
Kastanienallee 48, 10119

Freibad Plötzensee
Nordufer 26, 13351
strandbad-ploetzensee.de

Freischwimmer
Vor dem Schlesischen Tor 2a,
10997
freischwimmer-berlin.com

Galerie Camera Work
Kantstraße 149, 10623
camerawork.de

Galerie Christian Nagel
Weydingerstraße 2/4, 10178
galerie-nagel.de

Galerie Max Hetzler
Oudenarder Straße 16–20, 13347
maxhetzler.com

Gartenkolonie Freudental
Dubliner Straße, 13349

Gestalten Space
Sophienstraße 21, 10178
gestalten.com/space

Giro d'Espresso
Knobelsdorffstraße 47, 14059
giro-despresso.de

Goo
Oderberger Straße 45, 10435
paulsboutiqueberlin.de

Goodies
Warschauer Straße 69, 10243
goodies-berlin.de

Gottlob
Akazienstraße 17, 10823

Green Door
Winterfeldtstraße 50, 10781
greendoor.de

Hamburger Bahnhof
Invalidenstraße 50, 10557
hamburgerbahnhof.de

Hausbrauerei Eschenbräu
Triftstraße 67, 13353
eschenbraeu.de

Heimat
Kastanienallee 13–14, 10435
heimat-berlin.eu

Il Casolare
Grimmstraße 30, 10967

Jewish Museum
Lindenstraße 9–14, 10969
jmberlin.de

Johann Rose
Pannierstraße 41, 12047
johannrose.de

Jolesch
Muskauer Straße 1, 10997
jolesch.de

KaDeWe
Tauentzienstraße 21–24, 10789
kadewe.de

Kaffeehaus Sowohlalsauch
Kollwitzstraße 88, 10435
tortenundkuchen.de

Kaiser Wilhelm Memorial Church
Breitscheidplatz, 10789
gedaechtniskirche-berlin.de/KWG

KaterHolzig
Michaelkirchstraße 23, 10179
katerholzig.de

Käthe Kollwitz Museum
Fasanenstraße 24, 10719
kaethe-kollwitz.de

Kaufbar
Gärtnerstraße 4, 10245
kaufbar-berlin.de

Korea Haus
Nazarethkirchplatz 45, 13345

Kühn Keramik
Yorckstraße 18, 10965
kuehn-keramik.com

Kulturbrauerei
Schönhauser Allee 36, 10435
kulturbrauerei.de

Kulturforum
Matthäikirchplatz, 10785
kulturforum-berlin.de

Kunsthaus Tacheles
Oranienburger Straße 54, 13437
kunsthaus-tacheles.de

Le Gang
Kastanienallee 75, 10435
legang.de

Lindengarten
Nordufer 15, 13353
lindengarten-wedding.de

Literaturhaus
Fasanenstraße 23, 10719
literaturhaus-berlin.de

Liv Emaille
Pappelallee 82, 10437
emaille-shop.de

Luisenbad Library
Travemünder Straße 2, 13357
berlin.de/citybibliothek

Martin-Gropius-Bau
Niederkirchnerstraße 7, 10963
gropiusbau.de

Mauerpark
Gleimstraße 55, 10437
mauerpark.info

Me Collectors Room
Auguststraße 68, 10117
me-berlin.com

Meierei
Kollwitzstrasse 42, 10405
meierei.net

Melting Point
Kastanienallee 55, 10119

Memorial to the Murdered Jews of Europe
Cora-Berliner-Straße 1, 10117
holocaust-mahnmal.de

Memory Vintage
Schwedter Straße 2, 10119
memoryberlin.com

Modulor
Prinzenstraße 85, 10969
modulor.de

Molinari & Ko
Riemannstraße 13, 10961

Morena Bar
Wiener Straße 60, 10999

Museum der Dinge
Core Tex Records 25, 10999
museumderdinge.de

Museum für Fotografie
Jebensstraße 2, 10623
smb.museum

My Cheesecake
Ludwigkirchstraße 10, 10719
mycheesecake.de

Neue Nationalgalerie
Potsdamer Straße 50, 10785
neue-nationalgalerie.de

Neugerriemschneider
Linienstraße 155, 10115
neugerriemschneider.com

No Fire, No Glory!
Rykestraße 45, 10405
nofirenoglory.de

Nola's am Weinberg
Veteranenstraße 9, 10119
nola.de

optiKing
Eberswalder Straße 34, 10437
optiking.de

Paris Bar
Kantstraße 152, 10623
parisbar.net

Paul's Boutique
Oderberger Straße 47, 10435
paulsboutiqueberlin.de

Prater Garten
Kastanienallee 7-9, 10435
pratergarten.de

Prinzessinnengarten
Prinzessinnengarten, 10969
prinzessinnengarten.net

Pro QM
Almstadtstraße 48-50, 10119
pro-qm.de

Reichstag
Platz der Republik, 11011
bundestag.de

Rogacki
Wilmersdorfer Straße 145/146,
10585
rogacki.de

St Gaudy
Gaudystraße 1, 10437
gaudycafe.com

Sammlung Scharf-Gerstenberg
Schloßstraße 70, 14059
smb.museum

Sankt Oberholz
Rosenthaler Straße 72a, 10119
sanktoberholz.de

Schloß Bellevue
Spreeweg 1, 10557
berlin.de

Schwarzes Café
Kantstraße 148, 10623
schwarzescafe-berlin.de

Schwarzwaldstuben
Tucholskystraße 48, 10117
schwarzwaldstuben-berlin.com

Sing Blackbird
Sanderstraße 11, 12047
singblackbird.com

Singuhr-Hörgalerie
Danziger Straße 101, 10405
singuhr.de

Solar
Stresemannstraße 76, 10963
solarberlin.com

SO36
Core Tex Records 190, 10999
so36.de

Sportantiquariat Matthias Drummer
Wilmersdorfer Straße 10, 10585
sportantiquariat.de

Stattbad Wedding
Gerichtstraße 65, 13347
stattbad.net

Stiftung Haus der Geschichte der BRD
Knaackstraße 97, 10435
hdg.de/berlin

Strandbad-Mitte
Kleine Hamburger Straße 16,
10117
strandbad-mitte.de

TassenKuchen
Malplaquetstrasse 33, 13347
tassenkuchen.com

Tausend
Schiffbauerdamm 11, 10117
tausendberlin.com

The Early Bird Hype
Rosa-Luxemburg-Straße 15,
10178
theearlybirdhype.net

Trödelmarkt Arkonaplatz
1 Arkonaplatz, 10435
troedelmarkt-arkonaplatz.de

Vanille & Marille
Hagelberger Straße 1, 10965
vanille-marille.de

White Trash
Schönhauser Allee 6–7, 10119
whitetrashfastfood.com

Who Killed Bambi?
Rosentahler Straße 69, 10119
whokilledbambi.org

Yuu Shop
Steinstraße 26, 10119
yuu-shop.de

BIKES SHOPS, CLUBS, RACES AND VENUES

For links to our racing and
training routes, please visit
citycyclingguides.com

Berlin On Bike
Knaackstraße 97, 10435
berlinonbike.de

Berlin Six Day
sechstagerennen-berlin.de

Call A Bike
callabike.de

Cicli Berlinetta
Schönfließer Straße 19, 10439
cicli-berlinetta.de

Faltrad Direktor
Goethestrasze 79, 10623
faltrad-direktor.de

Keirin Cycle Culture Café
Oberbaumstraße 5, 10997
keirinberlin.de

Pino Touren
Sigmaringer Straße 26, 10713
pinotouren.de

Rad-Kreuz
Hagelberger Straße 53, 10965
rad-kreuz.de

Radsport Heinze
Forsthausallee 26, 12437
radsport-heinze.de

Radsport-Museum Wünsdorf
Gutenbergstraße 1, 15806 Zossen

RTFs
rtf-guide.de

Tempelhofer Freiheit
tempelhoferfreiheit.de

Velothon Berlin
garmin-velothon-berlin.de

Villa Pasculli
Rheinstraße 45, 12161
pasculli.de

OTHER USEFUL SITES

Brandenburg Willy Brandt Airport
berlin-airport.de

Deutsche Bahn
bahn.com

Eurostar
eurostar.com

Thalys
thalys.com

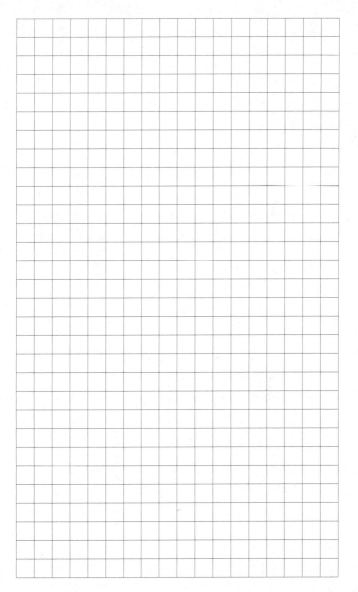

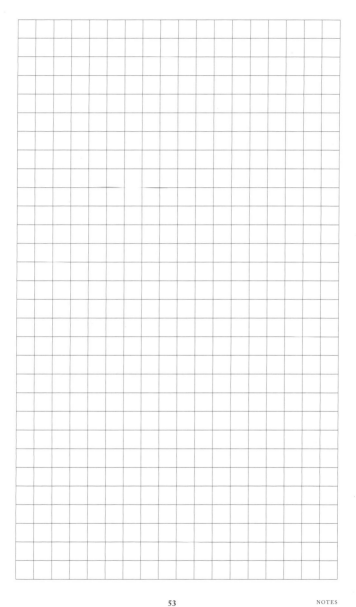

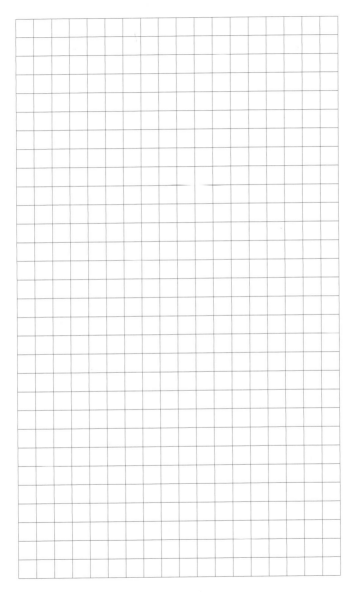

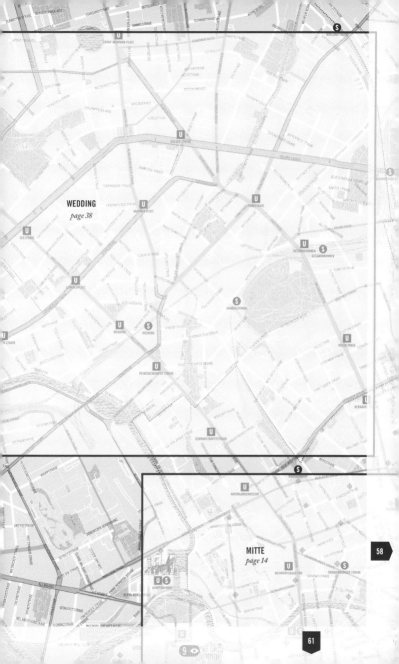

WEDDING
page 38

MITTE
page 14

PRENZLAUERBERG

page 20

MITTE

page 14

57

16

62

17

18

CHARLOTTENBURG
page 32

4

6 mins

½ km   ½ mile   1 km   1 mile

MITTE
page 14

KREUZBERG & KREUZKÖLLN
page 26

58

61

MITTE
page 14

15 👁

23 🚋

KREUZBERG & KREUZKÖLLN
page 26

24

28 👁

29 🍴

27 👁

Rapha, established in London, has always been a champion of city cycling – from testing our first prototype jackets on the backs of bike couriers, to a whole range of products designed specifically for the demands of daily life on the bike. As well as an online emporium of products, films, photography and stories, Rapha has a growing network of Cycle Clubs, locations around the globe where cyclists can enjoy live racing, food, drink and products. Rapha is also the official clothing supplier of Team Sky, the world's leading cycling team.

Rapha®